PERSONAL BRANDING

Master Your Digital Presence

By Felix Tih

ACKNOWLEDGEMENTS

I am deeply thankful to my lovely wife, Ayşenur Düzyol Tih for her loving support and for standing beside when I was writing this book. She also gave me space, the space to write and space to be. She has been my inspiration and motivation for continuing to improve my knowledge and move my career forward.

I also extend my gratitude to my siblings: Ntiabang, Betty Sebson and Fabien Tih. They were always present when I needed to discuss some ideas with them. They also supported and encouraged me in spite of all the time it took me away from the family.

I am grateful to all of those with whom I have had the pleasure to work during this and other projects.

Felix Tih

This book is designed to provide helpful information on the subjects discussed. I shared tips, and ideas to help you kick-start your online presence, but the effort you put in is what will make or break your success levels.

TABLE OF CONTENTS

Introduction

PART ONE
- Tips To Help in Building your Brand
- Identify Your Uniqueness and Your Strengths
- Own Your Space
- Share Your Knowledge
- Be Yourself
- Identify Your Values and Set Your Priorities

PART TWO
- Why You Need to Build a Personal Brand
- Successful Career
- To Improve in a Professional World
- Reputation Management
- Personal Executive Presence
- Thought Leadership

PART THREE
- Manage Your Reputation On and Offline
- Be Approachable, Well Mannered and Helpful in Everyday Activities
- Show Your Value
- Attend Industry Conferences and Trade Shows
- Manage Online and Offline Presence

- How to Stay Consistent

- How to Establish a Personal Brand
- Set Goals
- Benefits of Goal Setting
- Identify Your Target
- Unveil Your Talents and Expertise
- Establish a Communication Strategy

PART FOUR

- Personal Brand Definition
- Build an Audience of Influencers
- Align Your Social Networking Profiles
- Curate Great Content
- Write and Publish Great Content
- Give Until it Hurts

PART FIVE

- Ideas for Successful Personal Branding
- Discover
- Create
- Communicate
- Maintain
- Utilizing Social Media for Personal Branding
- Be Omnipresent: Create Multiple Streams of You
- Show Your Personality And Charm
- Add Value To The Conversation
- Be Interesting: Write, Video, Photograph, Share, Give
- Have Your Clients Blow Your Trumpet
- Find A Balance
- Be Social: Effectively Manage Your Social Systems
- Be Yourself And Let People Into Your Daily Life
- Be Remarkable: Do Something Worthy Of a Remark

PART SIX

- How to Manage Your Brand
- Self Appraisal
- Instant Impact
- Be the Brand You Want Others to See
- Allow Your Brand to Evolve With You
- Perseverance in Building Your Personal Brand
- Conclusion / About the Author

INTRODUCTION

Personal branding is about managing your name – even if you don't own a business – in a world misinformation, disinformation, and semi-permanent Google records. Going on a date? Chances are that your "blind" date has Googled your name. Going to a job interview? Ditto – Tim ferris

P ersonal branding involves managing your reputation, style, look, attitude and skill set the same way that a marketing team would run the brand for a bag of Doritos or bottle of shampoo. The idea is that you can develop a collection of symbols and associations with yourself, granting your name, face and work the same benefits that companies with solid brand equity (like Coca-Cola or Apple) enjoys.

There are some major differences between personal branding and branding for a company or product. For one, there are many dangers involved in using yourself as the face of your professional endeavors that are not present with a largely faceless larger company.

Personal branding is the process of developing a "mark" that is created around your name or your career. You use this "mark" to express and communicate your skills, personality, and values. We all can be a brand and cultivate our power to stand out and be unique. This uniqueness draws people to our product, our services, or even just our message. Your personal brand should be about who you are and what you have to offer.

Personal brands should be important to everyone. Personal brands are not only for the entrepreneur that owns their own business. It is the secret sauce that can make you stand out of a stack of resumes. If you don't develop your own personal brand, others will do it for you.

Developing your personal brand is the proactive way of controlling your career development and how you are perceived in the marketplace. A strong personal brand will impact your ability to get the right jobs, promotions, and increase your ability to attract talent and capital.

PART ONE

TIPS TO HELP IN BUILDING YOUR BRAND

Personal branding is a lot more than just optimizing your LinkedIn profile. Personal Branding has become an important concept in our day-to-day life in recent years.

It's important to build a personal brand because it's the only thing you're going to have. Your reputation online, and in the new business world is pretty much the game, so you've got to be a good person. You can't hide anything, and more importantly, you've got to be out there at some level. – Gary Vaynerchuk

Here are some questions to ask yourself before you kick-start your Personal Branding

What's my why?

Find your why. It is an important first step in figuring out how to achieve your goals and create a life you enjoy living. You must know why you do what you do or what you want to do. It is the best guide in crafting your Personal Brand. But you must know your audience.

Who needs to know what I do?

To market yourself, you must know how and where to find your target audience. You cannot afford to target everyone. You can compete with existing big brands by targeting a small and specific niche market or audience. Determine the people you want to impact and the content of your message.

What message do I want to pass across?

You must craft your message for a specific audience that is in line with your personal values.

What are my values?

Your values are the things that you believe are important in your life. They help you determine your priorities because your values highlight what you stand for. They represent your uniqueness and life goals.

What are my life goals?

Life goals are essentially everything you want to do in life. They are the things you'd like to achieve in order to be satisfied. Your life goals keep you on the right track, provide purpose and meaning, and a sense of fulfillment and communicate the right message.

Does my current brand communicate the right message?

Good communication is about getting the right message to the right person at the right time. You must reach your audience through the right communications channels because if you mix your signals, the reader or receiver may get confused and receive a message that you did not intend to send.

How does it fit with my personality or organization?

Personalities and organizations have different ways of communicating. Your communication should be in line with your personal and your organization's values.

Build a credible platform, including a website and social social media accounts that represent your brand and personality. You can use these platforms to share your voice.

Identify Your Uniqueness and Your Strengths

Think about the characteristics and strengths you've built in your career. If you are stuck, think about that "one thing" that everyone says you rock at. If you're still stuck, ask others.

Own Your Space

Once you've identified your uniqueness and strengths, perfect them. Learn all that you can and become the expert in that area. You can never stop learning. Read, absorb, and teach.

Share Your Knowledge

It's not enough to learn it; you have to teach it and share your knowledge by helping others. Do this through videos, social media, and writing both online and offline. This is where you prove you know your stuff and gain exposure from doing so.

Be Yourself

Find your own style. You don't have to do what everyone else is doing and just follow the crowd. Use your style and uniqueness to attract the jobs and clientele that you desire. Think of Gary Vaynerchuk and how he built his brand by making videos that share wine reviews and tips. No one else was doing it and now look around thousands of people are following in his footsteps. Find your own style and create a new set of footprints for others to follow in.

Identify Your Values and Set Your Priorities

It's important to have a clear picture of your personal and professional goals, both short and long-term. This will help you to not only identify the most important things to spend your time on but will also have something to align new projects with. Use your values and priorities as a compass that guides you both in action and your decision-making process. This will ensure you stay on track. Building a personal brand takes time and effort, but it's worth it. The need for a personal brand will continue to increase. It's the one thing that no one can take away from you, and it can follow you throughout your career. It's a leadership requirement that lets people know who you are and what you stand for.

PART TWO

WHY YOU NEED TO BUILD A PERSONAL BRAND

As society moves towards the digitalization of everything from shopping to social influence, the most valuable asset individuals can possess is a personal brand. Whether you're a 16-year-old high school student or a 40-year-old working in corporate America, regardless of whether or not you hate or love what you're doing, creating an online persona gives you credibility and visibility.

We live in an era where social media provides the chance to build a following. In many cases, people want to know who you are–who is the person behind your business? Knowing who you are can help your business seem more "real," even if you don't want to draw a line between your company brand and personal brand.

Successful Career

Having a personal brand can boost your company's visibility and bring more attention to your business. When you are seen as a thought leader or expert in your industry, this will naturally attract more eyeballs to your company. There's a reason why so many business leaders and entrepreneurs today make it a point to build their own personal brands and share their thoughts and experiences on a wide variety of platforms.

All of us are familiar with a business brand. It's the marketplace recognition of the promise of a company or professional services firm to meet or exceed the high expectations of its customers or clients in the delivery of products or services. Less familiar is a personal brand, which is the recognized promise of an individual to help a client or employer to be successful in their business.

Customers and clients buy from companies with

strong brands, such as Nike, Mercedes, Apple, Google and Starbucks, to name a few. These companies have a reputation for consistently offering high-quality products or services and delivering a great customer experience.

Companies with a great brand reputation are often not the lowest price offering in the marketplace but offer perceived value for the price charged. The strength of their brand gives these companies a competitive advantage. They become the preferred provider in their marketplace. They are the companies that customers and clients want to do business with, and they hold a significant market share within their market.

The same holds true for personal brands. Individuals develop a reputation such that clients want to do business with them. Employers want to promote them to their next job within the company or hire them as new employees or as consultants to provide an expert advice in a particular area. They differentiate themselves and develop a competitive advantage over their peers.

Ram V. Iyer of The Business Institute writes, "Personal branding is the intentional identification, packaging and marketing of a person's mission, strengths, capabilities, talents, background, appearance, etc. as a brand. A big objective of personal branding is to establish a specific image or impression of the person in the mind of others that evokes positive emotions."

Iyer continues, "If you build a strong personal brand, the benefits could increase your popularity, credibility, prestige, customer loyalty and market differentiation; it could attract new (and the right) clients, partners, employees and build bigger networks; and it could increase your perceived value (ability to charge higher prices) in the marketplace while negating your competition.

"Personal branding involves self-packaging – combining your mission, strengths, capabilities, talents, background, appearance, etc. – to define your uniqueness."- According to an article on bizjournals.com titled: Build your brand to achieve professional success.

So, as an individual, how do you build your personal brand?

✓ Do your job and do it well. Develop a reputation within your company, client base and industry as someone who achieves results, is a problem solver and facilitator with high emotional intelligence, is an individual who improves business processes and is someone who brings people together to find common ground.

✓ Develop your reputation as a thought leader – a recognized authority in your field of expertise. Get what you have accomplished and are accomplishing out in front of an audience. Volunteer to speak in front of groups. Help others be successful.

✓ Write articles or blogs on LinkedIn. Develop a website that can feature your articles and share your views on industry trends and on how to be an effective leader. Build an email list of individuals who would be interested in what you convey and send them what you write.

✓ Develop your networking skills. Attend industry conferences and network with other attendees. Your goal should not be to hand out as many business cards as possible at these events, but to develop relationships with a small number of attendees. Connect people with common interests or who can be helpful to each other. Become well known by others within your industry.

✓ Hone your leadership skills. Become known as an individual who creates a culture in which employees are empowered and encouraged to develop a sense of ownership in what they do. Develop a reputation for holding people accountable for results, as well as a boss people want to work for. Become known as someone who develops future leaders.

✓ Develop a reputation for honesty and integrity. People will not want to do business with people they don't trust. If you make a commitment to someone, be sure to keep that commitment.

✓ Always have and project the right attitude. It is a significant determinant of your success. Develop a reputation for seeing a world of possibilities and abundance, vs. seeing nothing but limitations and scarcity. Individuals with positive attitudes move forward in their career.

Always be on a journey to be the best in the world at what you do.

To Improve in a Professional World

In today's digital world, building your personal brand isn't a luxury, it's a necessity. And if you don't craft your personal brand by design, it'll be constructed by default.

With digital media, the 24/7/365, hyper-connected social media-enabled lifestyle nowadays, having a polished, professional personal brand is absolutely a necessity, not just for employees and job-seekers.

Personal branding is a critical part of how today's professionals present themselves; it shouldn't be left to others to define that personal brand. If you were developing and defining a business brand, you'd want to focus on the mission, purpose and value that brand signifies -- and the same is true for your personal brand.

If you're not defining your own brand, it's certain others are going to do that for you, so you need to take control of it. A good 77% of people you talk to are going to Google you to find out more information, and you need to make sure your personal brand reflects who you say you are, not who others say you are.

There are some areas you need to focus on to

improve in the professional world.

Reputation Management

The first area to address is your online reputation. There's an incredible amount of data available to anyone with just a few clicks, so make sure the information out there is accurate and -- to the extent that you can manage -- flattering to you. You always should claim your name regardless of whether or not you plan on creating your own website, and you always should maintain an "authority" site specific to you. This can be a personalized website or it can be your LinkedIn or other professional networking page.

Stay on top of search engine results so that you receive alerts every time you're mentioned or quoted.

Set a Google alert about yourself so you can keep track of what's being said about you, and of course, make sure your social media presence is showing your best, most polished and professional self.

Personal Executive Presence

This aspect of personal branding is less tangible, but just as important. Aligning your purpose, mission and values with your personal brand means first identifying what your purpose, mission and values are and how you can exemplify those in your daily life.

Personal executive presence is about having a clear vision and being able to communicate that vision; inspire and motivate others toward that same vision. It's about making sure your company's a great place to work and focusing on global success, and then making all these things known to the world at large.

Thought Leadership

Finally, establish yourself as a thought leader in whatever area you choose. This requires planning, strategy and execution; first to decide what space you want to "own," and how best to reach others within that space.

Be accessible as a source to the media. Make sure you're actively participating on social media in forums, Twitter chats, Facebook, LinkedIn posts,

Instagram etc... Be visible on your website. Sign up for speaking engagements, go to conferences, publicly take a stand on issues that affect your industry, your company and the areas you're interested in.

Personal branding isn't about exaggerating or showing off, it's about making sure that your best, most polished and professional self is accurately reflected in the public sphere.

This is about making the best impression possible to the most amount of people you can, before you even meet, before you interview, before you interact at all.

PART THREE

MANAGE YOUR REPUTATION ON AND OFFLINE

For most professionals, personal branding thrives online. Through juggling social media profiles, managing reputation, creating content, and securing our sites, we may forget that personal branding can also be done in person – and can be just as effective, if not more so.

Attending an industry event, association meeting, or even a professional cocktail hour in your city can be a great and easy way to transition the brand you've created online into the real world.

You know how important your online brand is, but there's just something about meeting others face-to-face, isn't there? Through a simple handshake, a conversation, or chance encounter, you're typically able to make a stronger connection than you would through technology.

One of the most important ways to develop your personal brand is to earn a great reputation. What people think of you and discuss about you can influence your personal brand — and support it as well.

Be dependable and consistent: Show up on time and deliver on what you promise. People should know what they can expect from you and that they can depend on you to pull through.

- ✓ Offer a great attitude: Be a positive, can do person that people want to work with.
- ✓ Show trustworthiness: Do the right thing, even when it's hard.
- ✓ Volunteer and be helpful: Show that you're always willing to help out.
- ✓ Take action: Be known as a doer, someone who gets things done dependably.
- ✓ Support your team: Be a team player and always be ready to help out your colleagues.
- ✓ Be known for something: What are you good at doing? Let everyone know! Don't be afraid to toot your own horn. If you don't promote yourself, who will?

Here are some ways you can manage your reputation.

Be Approachable, Well Mannered and Helpful in Everyday Activities

Want to build a memorable personal brand for yourself? Keep in mind the way you'd like others to see you on a daily basis. I believe putting out good karma can only lead to good things in life.

Show Your Value

You can extend your brand's reputation with your new connections by demonstrating how you're a valuable asset to their network. Try to listen and engage others more than talk about yourself – you may get a chance to offer your expertise or someone you know that is a right fit for the challenge.

Attend Industry Conferences and Trade Shows

Conferences provide several benefits to building your brand. First off, they introduce you to other professionals in your industry (and those whom you already "know" through online means) and help grow your network exponentially in a short period of time.

These events also enhance and add to your skill set by featuring expert speakers, vendors and exhibitioners in your field.

Striking a balance of online and offline interaction will sustain your personal brand in the long run.

Manage Online and Offline Presence

It can be difficult to gain your customers' trust in 2018 without an online presence. You know you need to be searchable on Google. However, with so many bloggers, influencers and companies clamoring to build a name for themselves on the internet, you need to invest considerable time to build up your brand online.

But what if you conduct most of your business offline? While a digital-only presence may be adequate for an online company, you will need an offline brand presence as well if you are a dentist, real estate agent, brick-and-mortar shop owner or work in more traditional industries that rely on in-person connections. Most of your customers will do some research on the internet before doing business with you, so you will need to build up a presence both on and offline that represents the value of your brand. Ideally, your online presence will serve to prepare future clients for what to expect while working with you in-person.

However, as you build your brand image, remember that people process information online differently than they do in-person. While your online brand might provide smaller doses of value over a longer term, many clients will weigh in-person meetings and offline advertising more heavily when they analyze your brand values.

For the longest time, everyone in marketing was talking about "offline and online brands" as if they were two different things. Thankfully those days are ending.

How to Stay Consistent

Use The Same Language In Online Copy And In Person

Your brand voice should be authentic but deliberate. It is likely that you naturally discuss topics that interest you offline. Your online voice should follow the same pattern. Online, you write about topics you care about, including your industry, hobbies and personal experience but with a slightly different style. Your writing may follow the way you speak so that it sounds natural, but remember that the spoken word is often much more casual than written messages.

Tailor your language to the platform you are using while maintaining a single message. For example, you may be able to use descriptive writing in a blog post but that same copy would not be useful for Twitter (unless you can keep it under 280 characters!). Make sure your online brand personality matches who you are in person, so you stay authentic and consistent across both.

Leverage User-Generated Content Online

Your online presence is a way for prospects and customers to get to know you before meeting you in person. Certain aspects of working with you can be difficult to share in-person and are better suited to your social pages or your website. Usually, this content is "user-generated," meaning it comes directly from customers who have already worked with you in the past. A few examples of user-generated content you can share online are:

- ✓ Online reviews
- ✓ User testimonials
- ✓ Recommendations from colleagues
- ✓ Customer videos or photos

This kind of content allows prospects to learn what it is like to work with you from the perspective of past customers. It can be challenging to share this kind of material in an offline meeting (you might come across as a little self-centered), but many potential customers will appreciate the chance to learn more about you from another point of view.

Deepen Online Relationships With Offline Engagements

Although online engagement is an effective way to build rapport with prospects, you may find that nothing replaces an in-person meeting. In practice, you should try to connect these two sides of your personal brand as much as possible -- turn online conversations into phone conversations or coffee meetings or even find a way to present on your favorite topic at a conference. Your online presence should help turn you into a thought leader for your given industry, meaning more people will reach out to you when they need an opinion on that topic.

Think of your online brand as your marketing team, while your offline brand is sales. Your online brand advocates for you even when you're not there. Anything you upload is always available for anyone to consume, but each piece of content leaves only a small impact. However, your online materials might convince someone to take the next step and contact you for a meeting. Your offline presence packs a bigger punch. An in-person meeting usually seals the deal, but you can't be in more than one place at once, so you have to be deliberate with who you meet. If your online brand accurately represents who you are in person, it can help bring you more qualified leads, even when you're out in the field.

How to Establish a Personal Brand

When people say, "I want to build a personal brand," the first thing they think about is numbers. Number of Twitter, LinkedIn & Instagram followers, Facebook Likes, blog subscribers etc... Those are very poor metrics for building a meaningful personal brand.

Building a personal brand means providing so much value in one (or multiple) niche(s) that people begin to associate your name with the idea of what it means to be successful in that industry. You become a thought leader and an influencer.

Considering how important your personal brand is to your career, your business and even personal happiness, it's remarkable how little time we spend on something that can be so meaningful. But the importance of marketing yourself, whether as an entrepreneur or as a valuable member of the workforce, is becoming abundantly clear. Building a personal brand is an investment in yourself and your future.

Here are some pointers on how to establish your personal brand.

Set Goals

Just because it's a personal brand doesn't mean you should wing it. Set solid quarterly goals. Begin with tangible goals for your own performance. Decide how often you will share brand-appropriate content on your social media channels, how often you'll post on your blog or, if relevant, share email updates on projects. Apply the research you gathered from influencers you admire and make a list of definitive goals with hard numbers. "Post on my blog more" is not a goal. "Post on my blog two times per week" is a goal.

In the second quarter, start to shift your goal focus to external metrics. How many followers do you want to hit? At what rate do you want your audience to grow? What can you do to achieve that? Once you've built the foundation for your presence by achieving the goals you set in the first quarter, you can begin to tailor it to your reception. Make note of when you hit certain goals and don't view any missed milestones as failures but, instead, as learning experiences. Not only will this allow you to flesh out your messaging, but it'll keep you focused and informed for building future strategies.

Benefits of Goal Setting

✓ Goal setting helps you get clear on what you want.

✓ Goal setting helps you identify what distractions may be blocking your success.

✓ Goal setting, including writing your goals, helps program your subconscious mind and activate mental powers that will enable you to accomplish these goals.

✓ Goal setting helps motivate you, especially when you get overwhelmed in today's fast-paced society.

✓ Goal setting leads to success, increased income, and greater career/life happiness.

Identify Your Target

Before you can communicate your personal brand to the right people, you must identify who needs to know about you and what you have to offer. They are the people and companies that are just waiting to experience and appreciate your brand.

One of the biggest mistakes that budding personal branders make is trying to appeal to everyone. Think about the game of darts: You have to aim in order to hit the board. (If you let your darts go without aiming them, you probably won't be very popular.) If you hit the board, you score. And if your aim is very good and you hit the bull's eye, even better!

You know that defining a target audience is a business best practice. But defining a target audience is a best practice for anyone that needs others to give them something. It might be a salary, an investment or money in exchange for a product or service. Whenever you need something from someone you go through at least some of the steps in defining a target audience.

We go through the target audience process even at an early age. Think back to when you were a kid. When you wanted a treat you went through the target audience process. You knew that your mom probably wouldn't be the one to approve your request so you went to your dad and you made sure to catch him in the right mood.

That's an example of defining your target audience. It's a basic example, but businesses go through that process so they have more success. It doesn't make sense to try to please everyone. Your time, energy and money are better invested in a target audience. And that goes for defining the target audience for your personal brand too.

There are basically three people that fit into your personal brand's target audience:

- ✓ The Person That Will Pay You.
- ✓ The Person That Influences The Person That Pays You.
- ✓ Your Supporter.

The first person on the list, the one that pays you, is your main focus. This might be your current boss or your next boss or your clients. It might be the target customer of your current business or your next business. It could also be an investor or a bank.

Identify the person that is in charge of the next step in your career. It might be an investor. It might be a client. Or it could be your boss. It could be a specific person that you have in mind or it could be the vision of a person. Whatever it is, identify that person and move on.

Next, create a complete description of the person.

Marketers and business leaders do this all the time with their customers. They put comprehensive descriptions together of their target customers to create detailed, vivid images of the exact person their employees will think about when making every decision in the business.

Unveil Your Talents and Expertise

How amazing is it if a person is associated with a brand? In the context of products, we know well what a brand means to a company as well as to us. Any product or service to make itself relevant and likeable, needs a unique identity which is created through branding. In the same way, people like us to be identified as personalities, and are nowadays getting linked to or creating their own brand, what is known as 'Personal Branding'.

Personal Branding simply means advertising a person's skills, abilities, talents and positive reviews through various mediums established in order to get himself/herself noticed by all. In short, it is used to differentiate you from everybody else and is about defining yourself to your various audiences and increasing your credibility amongst them; it also interprets correctly as to what it is that other people seek from you, or that attained value only you have command over, which would further help to establish your name amongst your co-workers, colleagues and customers.

Personal Branding is not only about how to handle your image, and sustain it over a period of time;. however, what everybody wants to is to be 'authentic' and pursue your work in a way which makes its authenticity evident in whatever you do.

Your personal brand is not just an image; in fact, it's a commitment which defines you and moreover, it is the expectation which everybody has of you and which you can set forth through your accountability.

Some people would say that 'Personal Branding' is a way to 'Show Off"; that creating a personal brand and a name for themselves are just ways to show off to the world what they've got and that no one is better than them. Well, I am not saying that praising one's skills and achievements is wrong, but the important thing I believe is to maintain that 'authenticity' in it, and not just merely say these things for showing off as everybody is equally good in their own way. Indeed, personal branding of the self is an ongoing process which ultimately lets you learn and grow and to be more self-aware, in creating a unique you.

Bringing on your personal brand means the real 'you', comprising of your own skills and driven by your inner passion, which ultimately defines you and delivers to you a sense of accomplishment.

When you are wholly driven by your passion and master a certain skill, you tend to become the owner of a specific task that can be done only by you, which increases your chances to be referred among people. Coming in contact with your skills and talents, people tend to value you, which in turn increases your credibility.

Establish a Communication Strategy

Having strong communication skills is crucial. One needs to know when it's important to listen and when its necessary to respond. There are many subtleties in communication that can influence others; the best communicators strengthen their personal brand using speech and silence to influence others' opinion of them. They intuitively know "when silence is golden" and how to "read between the lines". They have strong emotional intelligence, and choose the right words and use them at the right time.

Smart personal branding can help you communicate your unique value proposition and enable you to become a thought leader both within and outside your company.

Key elements of your personal brand communication plan.

PART FOUR

PERSONAL BRAND DEFINITION

Draft a short, biographical statement that summarizes your brand. The language here is important and will be useful in crafting your social networking profiles.

Personal branding is the practice of marketing people and their careers as brands. It is an ongoing process of developing and maintaining a reputation and impression of an individual, group, or organization.

Build an Audience of Influencers

Identify your target audience (s) based on the following categories:

✓   Influencers that inform and inspire you – Make a list of all the people (writers, thinkers, artists, filmmakers, columnists, journalists, athletes, clients and organizations) that influence you and your view of the world and from whom you draw creative energy and insight.

✓   Influencers in your peer group – Make a list of the influencers and thought-leaders in your space. You want to get to know these people and have them know you.

✓   Influencers you don't know yet – Obviously, you can't list these (because you don't know them yet), but think about where they might be and open yourself to discovering them when they reveal themselves. Remember, influencers come in all shapes and sizes and everyone has a network within which there may be value for you.

Align Your Social Networking Profiles

Create or update your profiles on popular social networking sites using the biographical information you created in item 1 above and an exceptional photograph. Focus on the following sites in the following order:

✓ Twitter – Establish a personal (@yourname) account and start following the influencers in item 2 above (many of them are on Twitter).

✓ LinkedIn – Update your profile using your biography created above and use the same photo that you use on your other social profiles.

✓ Facebook – Facebook is an important platform. Create a page / group to interact with the public.

✓ Instagram: Share pictures and videos. Combine your private and professional account.

✓ Tiktok : TikTok is a video-sharing social networking service.

Create Great Content

Develop your skills for finding and sharing great "on brand" content in your social networks. Always look for "evergreen" content that doesn't quickly get stale and adds value. Focus on the following sharing frequencies in your networks:

✓ Twitter: Share more frequently, several to many times per day.

✓ LinkedIn: Share great articles once or twice a week to as much as once or twice per day.

✓ Facebook: Easy interaction with audience and followers.

✓ Instagram & TikTok: Share pictures and videos stories.

Write and Publish Great Content

It's hard to develop a personal brand and build thought leadership without writing or otherwise expressing your views.

Develop an editorial calendar for blog posts and other "shareable" content, such as presentations, articles, etc., that can be repurposed from content you are already producing. Publish in existing publications or establish a blog.

Give Until it Hurts

Dedicate time each day and each week to paying attention to your influencers in social networks. Review Tweets and shares of key influencers and "like" them or share them or add comments. Promote others as your main strategy for promoting your own personal brand.

Personal branding is never one-size-fits-all. Adapt your strategy to your personality.

PART FIVE

IDEAS FOR SUCCESSFUL PERSONAL BRANDING

Your online identity is powerful. Your personal brand becomes the image you portray to your world of online follows. If you want to leverage it as a tool to advance your professional growth, you need to monitor and guard it closely.

Personal branding helps you stay very productive because you can focus on projects you enjoy and have a sense of purpose and passion behind them.

There are many other benefits for personal brands, such as the ability to demand a premium price, just like Donald Trump has done with the ties and steaks that wear his name. Also, you gain greater visibility and acknowledgment for your work and opportunities that your peers won't be able to maintain.

Here are some steps you should take to achieve personal branding success:

Discover

In order to really understand who you are and carve out a career path moving forward, investing in self-discovery is critical. In fact, if you don't spend time learning about yourself, your values, personal mission, and unique attributes, you will be at a disadvantage when marketing your brand to others. Start by removing yourself from distractions and ask yourself, "Who am I?" and, "If I could do anything, what would it be?" Also, when discovering your brand, you'll want to lay out a development plan for yourself, that includes your current situation and your goals broken down in intervals, from one year to twenty years in the future. It's extremely important to have a destination in your head and on paper before proceeding to create your brand in step two. The most successful individuals will be able to merge their passion with expertise, so that they have the fuel needed to push through adversity, and the skills required to solve customers problems. Also, selecting an unsaturated niche that you can claim during this stage is significant for positioning your brand as unique.

Create

Creating your personal brand is all about forming marketing materials that position you as extraordinary in your niche. When I was at college, I used to bring a resume, cover letter, CD portfolio, references document, and business card with me to interviews. I even had my own promotional website. With the rise of web 2.0 and all of these social media tools, we can get far more creative these days. For instance, now you can create a blog, or a video resume on YouTube or a LinkedIn profile to separate yourself from the other individuals applying for the same jobs as you. The point of creating your brand is to have several materials online and offline that can help sell you. They are all used as talking points that can get a conversation started between you and your audience. Online, they tell your audience more about what you do, what you offer and the benefits of working with you. Offline, they are used in situations where people need a visual display of your brand.

Identify what gets you up in the morning. What drives you to change the world? Look at every person who has a successful personal brand and you can immediately identify what drives them. For Elon Musk, it's technological innovation; for Sheryl Sandberg, it's advancing women in the workforce;

for Tim Cook, it's design and engineering; and for Oprah Winfrey, it's self-betterment and social good.

While their messaging extends beyond these topics, audiences are committed to these personalities because they are truly passionate about the things that drive them.

Hence, you should create your personal brand taking into consideration that which drives you.

Communicate

Now it's time to use everything you've created to let people know you exist. The communication stage is focused on allowing you to gain the necessary visibility to be recruited based on your passion or what people readily see online. There are many direct and indirect methods of attaining this visibility, such as commenting on blogs or attending in-person networking events in your industry. You can even do some freelance writing for magazines, newspapers, online websites and blogs to get your name out there. When it comes to your own blog, if you build it, they won't come. You have to find way to attract your audience, which could mean joining forums, interviewing experts, starting a newsletter, networking with people in your industry and much more. In this step, you'll want to put on your "personal PR" hat and leverage your materials to pitch the press, which includes bloggers and traditional journalists now.

Maintain

As you grow, mature, and accelerate in your career, everything you've created has to be updated and accurately represent the current "brand you." It's very easy to be careless with your online brand, leaving your websites months or even years old or your LinkedIn profile positioning you as an intern, instead of a marketing manager. Going back to everything you created and updating it with fresh information is critical. Also, you need to monitor your brand online to ensure all conversations about you are factual. Brand maintenance also captures reputation management, where you have to own your Google results by ensuring that you have the right social networking profiles setup and monetized, as well as enough content created or press mentions to own the top ten results for your name in Google.

Utilizing Social Media for Personal Branding

Like a corporate brand that represents a particular business entity, a personal brand is a manifestation of "you" on an individual level. But not everyone can successfully pull this off. If you've been struggling to build your personal brand, social media is where you should begin.

Branding used to be the concern of large businesses only, but with social media, any business can easily build their personal brand. Personal branding allows you to humanise your company and differentiate yourself from the competition.

When building your personal brand online you have to establish yourself as an authority and create a trustworthy voice that will attract businesses and employers. There are different personal branding tools all over the internet that will help you through the course of branding yourself right; however, using effective strategies is the way to go to sustain and build a stronger market especially when announcing your newest startup.

Sharing online allows you to create an online identity that echoes your own ideals and professional expertise. Patience is part of the process.

Social media has become a key branding tool for professionals across all fields, including real estate. Brokers and agents can connect with fellow industry players, push out information about listings or open houses and use social listening tools to identify potential clients who may be looking to buy.

But as with any brand, no one will want to follow you if all you post about is business. Your social media audience wants to know that there's a human being behind your accounts, and it's important to have a healthy mix of personal and professional content to keep people engaged.

Here are key ways to use social media as an effective brand-building tool without alienating your followers.

Be Omnipresent: Create Multiple Streams of You

Many people think that a Facebook page is where you start and finish. In fact it is only one of many. The best place to start is with a web presence that you own and that is your own blog with its own domain name and self hosted. To really be truly ubiquitous there are some other social media channels you should contemplate if you are really serious and passionate about developing and promoting brand "You". These include a YouTube Channel for your videos, Instagram for your pictures, Slideshare for your presentations, Twitter for communication, immediacy and promoting your content globally, LinkedIn for the corporate networking opportunities and of course Facebook. You need to keep in mind that the opportunities are now global and the challenge is to always be thinking a global village and digital.

Show Your Personality And Charm

You may be focused on selling your product and service, but it is paramount that you incorporate the importance of intangible factors like personality and charm. You've been in sales your whole life because every day you are selling your most important asset: yourself.

It may sound cliché, but people do business with people they like. So sell yourself; the business will come later.

Add Value To The Conversation

Whether you use social media or not, it is critical to understand that your brand is already being talked about online. By using social media, you can steer the conversation in the direction you desire. The No. 1 rule of social media is to provide value. Always make sure you're adding value to the conversation while keeping the goals of your audience in mind.

Be Interesting: Write, Video, Photograph, Share, Give

Most of us are quite interesting and we need to let everyone know that. Some us are a bit shy at a cocktail party but hanging with your friends it is a different story. So document your experiences whether that be with photos, videos or what you write. Take that day to day documentation of your thoughts and media and put more of it online.

Have Your Clients Blow Your Trumpet

Some brokers/agents use social media to engage with their customers and use that as a brand building tool. It adds more validity to your skills when praise comes from your clients rather than yourself. Tagging your clients in a post mentioning a successful closing might be the first step to brand building on social media.

Find A Balance

It's important for your social media to be a reflection of yourself, personality and all. But at the same time, remember who your audience is. Your followers are likely interested in your real estate knowledge, not necessarily how you feel about the current political climate. Make sure to find a balance or people might not take you seriously in the real estate industry.

Be Social: Effectively Manage Your Social Systems

Once you have these multiple social media channels you then need to manage and optimize them to continue to put your personal brand in front of as many people as possible that displays your knowledge, credibility and influence in the most professional manner possible. LinkedIn can be optimized with up to three web addresses and you can now also add your Twitter and Blog feed to your home page. On Twitter you can follow people in your industry niche and link your Twitter homepage to your blog or website.

Be Yourself And Let People Into Your Daily Life

Don't be afraid to let people in on your daily life. If you post little snippets of your life, people will love following you. Keep your social media positive — happy pictures of your friends and family, and then sprinkle in a little bit of work-related subjects. Be real! When you make people laugh, they will be glued to your reality.

Be Remarkable: Do Something Worthy Of a Remark

Most of us want to play it safe and stick to what we know but this doesn't create a life that gets talked about or something that gets shared.

PART SIX

HOW TO MANAGE YOUR BRAND

Many organizations want to be known as the best at what they do. They want their brand to stand on its own without any explanation, and they want their brand identity to align with their brand image. Think, Coca-Cola, Jaguar, Tesla, Google, Apple, Chipotle, etc.

But, it can take years to build a solid brand – from logo creation, to the company mission statement, and the strategies used to deploy content. All these items require brand strategy, patience and thought to create. On the flip side, it could only take moments to ruin a brand.

Somewhere among the complex digital web, your company brand is out there representing everything you stand for. But, it can also pose as a liability if not managed correctly. Just one wrong use of the logo could even be catastrophic.

You are just as much a brand as Google, Pepsi or John Lewis and as such, you need to present and market yourself in a similar manner. I believe that your personal brand should be personal. It should be authentic, and it should be a rich representation of not only what you've done, but of who you are and what you care about.

What makes you unique and what do you want people to remember about you? Identify your Unique Selling Proposition (USP) and use it to market your personal expertise. This involves creating a narrative that communicates what you stand for and the value you bring to the table/project/ organisation and identifies your strengths and talents to managers, colleagues and peers.

Self Appraisal

The ancient Greek aphorism "know thyself" is the starting point for personal branding. Effective performance at work depends on self-awareness as to how you behave, react and learn. It is crucial that you recognise and acknowledge your personal values and beliefs, strengths, weaknesses, motivators and how they affect your work and development.

It helps to seek feedback from those who know you, it is helpful in developing greater effectiveness. Start by asking for feedback around things you do that others appreciate, value, or think you do well and want to see you doing or do more of. You may be surprised by some of what you hear. Then you can think about what you want to do differently.

Self-awareness is important because it is directly linked to effectiveness at work and in your personal life. Research shows that emotional intelligence is often a greater predictor of effectiveness than IQ. The focus of IQ is task-oriented while the emphasis of emotional intelligence is on people and relationships.

Instant Impact

Build your personal brand on this realistic self-appraisal so that you are able to see yourself as a product and manage what is recognisable about yourself. Awareness of what others see help you identify blind spots and deal with practical problems or self-projection. Research shows that you have up to five seconds to make an impact. Consider three questions:

✓ What do you want people to say about you?
✓ What do people perceive when you join the conversation?
✓ Is your brand congruent with and representative of your aspirations?

If you describe yourself as an excellent communicator, competent, and detail orientated – is that representative of how you look, sound and behave? Are you punctual? Is there a button missing from your cuff? If you are late can you explain fluently, convincingly and charmingly why you were late? In other words – are you on message?

Aim to actively live up to your personal brand statement and to show off that brand. Self-esteem is about how you see yourself and personal branding is about how others see you.

Be the Brand You Want Others to See

Simply put, if you want to be recognized as philanthropic, then be big-hearted and generous. If you want to be perceived as humble, then be humble. Your brand directly reflects what you've done, who you are, and what you care about.

Allow Your Brand to Evolve With You

It's no secret that the only constant in life is change. As you learn and grow, so will your brand. Let it. Just be cognizant of what the changes are. Most importantly, realize that rough patches and hard times—whether they be layoffs, health crises, or family emergencies—don't have to define your brand, but they can refine it.

If someone were to "Google" you today or ask your friend or boss about you, would they discover something different from what you want your brand to be? Be honest with yourself. When what you want your brand to be is inconsistent with the perceptions of others, the only person who has the power to change it is you. There is strength in knowing who you are and working every day to make it real.

Perseverance in Building Your Personal Brand

Personal branding takes time. It is probably the most important thing – it's something you're always building with your eyes firmly on long term goals.

Sure it's not going to take you five years to build a personal brand, but it is the long-term commitment to it that really counts. Personal branding isn't something you do to get the next job. Jobs come and go.

Personal branding is about defining who you are and what you stand for, and it takes years to nurture and build. I know, I've been doing it for a decade and I'll never stop, because I know it's the most important thing I can do to build the future I want. Incidentally, even though I'm not looking for one, based on the job offers coming my way, it's also being recognized as a powerful asset by recruiters. The world is shifting and businesses are starting to understand this new digital world.

I cannot emphasize this enough. Building a strong, focused personal brand is the tool of careers today. It's the tool of building dreams. A personal brand is a powerful investment to make in yourself.

Personal branding is about marketing yourself, improving yourself, and using the brand you as a launching platform to follow your dreams and do what you want to.

Whether it takes you 1 month, 2 years, or over 30 years, the time spent working towards your goal is worth it. Not only because the time spent doing it increases your knowledge, value and brand, but the integrity and life experience you gain can't be replaced.

Online profiles such as LinkedIn never sleep. Whatever you've made public is available 24/7. The information you've published on the web, either through status updates or blog posts, is always waiting either to lurk or shine. What would you have it do? The best part of taking an active part in "getting it" by working hard and reaping the benefits of when you "got it" is that you have the tools in your belt to shape what you'd be known for.

Conclusion

To have a prosperous business, you must understand the power of branding. Your personal brand is made up of the qualities and unique traits you relay about yourself, and it represents the way you want other people to think about you.

Personal Branding has become more talked about these days as individuals seek to differentiate themselves by developing a unique brand that will propel career and job opportunities. Many people think that personal branding is just for celebrities, but every individual is in fact, a brand.

There are millions of other people offering the same service as you, now ask yourself; how do I currently stand out in the crowd?

Without branding, you're simply part of the many, and not part of the few.

Personal Branding is about really digging deep and spending time developing a unique Brand Statement, Brand Position, Name (that speak to what you're doing), Brand Promise, USP (Unique Selling Proposition) and Graphic imagery. Think of your Brand as a stage, it allows you to rise above the rest and show consumers with confidence why they should choose you versus your competitor.

As a brand, you can leverage the same strategies that

make celebrities or corporate brands appeal to your consumers. Personal Branding involves four basic traits: unique capabilities, positioning, values, and a brand promise. Just like a corporate brand, you must establish and project what makes you unique and why people should come to you rather than the next guy.

The single biggest mistake people make is that they either brand themselves just for the sake of doing it, or they fail to see the value from investing in building a strong brand foundation, before rushing into marketing and advertising. By investing the time and resources on properly and effectively branding yourself, you will attract the right opportunities.

The Social online world is the same as in person, so you need to follow the same rules of engagement: Learn to listen (start a discussion) and earn the right to be heard (share your expertise and tools).

Social Media impressions are very important so be invariable in your messaging, and always be transparent, it creates authenticity. Create a succinct tone for your LinkedIn, Instagram, Twitter and Facebook profiles, your email signature, blog and promotional materials - your messaging can have a huge impact on your professional image.

You can also monitor your personal brand name across the web with Google Alerts, a free tool which sends e-mail updates about a topic or phrase that you choose. With focus, and a well developed brand strategy, you will have set the foundation and mapped out the path to becoming a successful personal Brand.

Social Media handles:

Twitter: https://twitter.com/TihFelixx

LinkedIn: https://www.linkedin.com/in/felixtih

Facebook: https://www.facebook.com/felixtih

Instagram: https://www.instagram.com/felixtih

Thank you

Published by Kindle ebook

ASIN: B07MMVGQ6N